Narad Muni
and the Benefit of the Company of a Sadhu

Adapted from a story told by Sant Ram Singh Ji on August 8, 2016

Illustrated by Carlos Brito

GO JOLLY
BOOKS

Narad Muni and the Benefit of the Company of a Sadhu

Narad Muni and The Benefit of the Company of a Sadhu
is a story originally told in a Satsang by Sant Ram Singh Ji on August 8, 2016 during a Meditation Retreat Program at RadhaSwami Ashram, Channasandra Village, Karnataka, India.

Special thanks to those who reviewed & critiqued the story:
Graham Leavett-Brown, Richard & Sharon Malarich.
Their suggestions have made the adult story
more appropriate for children.

Translated by Ashok Shinkar
Transcribed by Ali Czernin, Geoff Halstead, & Harvey Rosenberg

Extra thanks to Carlos Brito, our illustrator, whose use of color and his skills at creating whimsical characters make this a delightful visual journey for children and adults. His illustrations make our hearts dance with joy & gratitude.

ISBN-13: 978-1-942937-17-3

(c) 2017 All Rights Reserved

Published by
Go Jolly Books
www.gojollybooks.com
74 Gem Ln., Sandpoint, ID 83864 USA

FIRST EDITION, GO JOLLY BOOKS, First Printing 2017
10 9 8 7 6 5 4 3 2 1 Printed in the U.S.A.

Narad Muni
and the Benefit of the Company of a Sadhu

Adapted from a story told by Sant Ram Singh Ji on August 8, 2016

INTRODUCTION

In January, 2014, at RadhaSwami Ashram, Channasandra Village, Karnataka, India, Sant Ram Singh Ji gave me permission to take stories He told in Satsang and publish them as books.

He told me to make sure the books were for children. This meant I could change His words directed to adults to words more suitable for children. With His Limitless Grace, reviewers of the first five books have told us children like the books.

Narad Muni and the Benefit of the Company of a Sadhu
shows the importance of spending as much time as possible with a Living Sant Mat Master.

It's a beautiful story demonstrating that the Love we receive from a Living Master,
the Grace we receive from a Living Master,
the Friendship we receive from a Living Master,
all the Gifts we receive from a Living Master, are impossible to receive anywhere except in the company of a Living Master until we have gone within.

Vibrant illustrations of joyful color combinations create whimsical characters that complement the words and make it a story book that will have a deep impact on children. We hope you enjoy it.

Radhaswami,
Harvey Rosenberg

Narad Muni
and the Benefit of the Company of a Sadhu

Adapted from a story told by Sant Ram Singh Ji on August 8, 2016

Dedication

This book is dedicated to Sant Ram Singh Ji,
a Sant Mat Master Whose Limitless Grace makes it possible to live in this world of sorrow and joy with complete faith that our Master will take our soul back to God someday.
He is our only True Friend.

Once upon a time, Narad Muni wondered, "What is the benefit of the company of a sadhu?"

He went to Vaikuntha, the celestial home of Lord Vishnu, and asked Lord Vishnu this question.

Lord Vishnu looked at him and laughed to himself. He felt that, "Narad Muni is himself a sadhu and he is asking me this question?"

He told Narad Ji, "Go down to Earth to this particular town. Go to the east of town and you will see a tree. There is an insect below this tree that makes balls of cow dung and then stores them near the tree. Go there and ask your question."

Narad Muni got annoyed by the answer, and told Lord Vishnu, "You always make fun of me whenever I ask you questions. I'm asking you this question and you're not answering me. You're telling me to ask an insect this question but I don't even know how to talk to that insect."

Lord Vishnu said, "Just go. There is a well there. Next to the well is the tree and, below that tree, you will find the insect. When you see it, ask your question."

Narad Muni agreed, and followed Lord Vishnu's directions to the location of the well and the tree, east of the town, where he indeed saw an insect carrying a ball of cow dung.

When Narad Muni saw this insect, he folded his hands and very humbly asked, "Oh insect, please tell me. What is the benefit of meeting a sadhu?"

As soon as he asked this question, the insect looked at Narad Muni and died.

Very surprised, Narad Muni thought there must be something wrong about my question that caused the insect to die. Sad at heart, he went back to Lord Vishnu and related what happened.

Lord Vishnu said, "Come back here after about four months, and we will find a solution."

After four months, Narad Muni, who was adamant about getting his question answered, returned to Lord Vishnu.

Lord Vishnu told him, "Okay, return to that same place. On that tree, you will find a nest with a one-month-old baby swan in it. Go there, and ask that swan your question."

Narad Muni went back to the place and found the tree with the nest containing the baby swan.

And again, with folded hands, he asked, "Oh bird, what is the benefit you get by meeting a sadhu?"

The small bird looked at him and fell to the ground, dead.

Seeing this, Narad Muni was aghast and deeply saddened. He was concerned that there was something seriously wrong in the question he was asking.

When he returned to Lord Vishnu, Narad Muni related the whole incident.

Lord Vishnu told him, "Okay, come back in ten months and I will give you your answer."

After ten months, Narad Muni came to him and, again, asked that question.

Lord Vishnu replied, "Go to that same city, but go to the palace of the king. He has a newborn baby. Ask the baby that question."

This really upset Narad Muni, who said to Lord Vishnu, "First, you directed me to ask an insect my question, and that insect died. Since the insect had no family, that was okay."

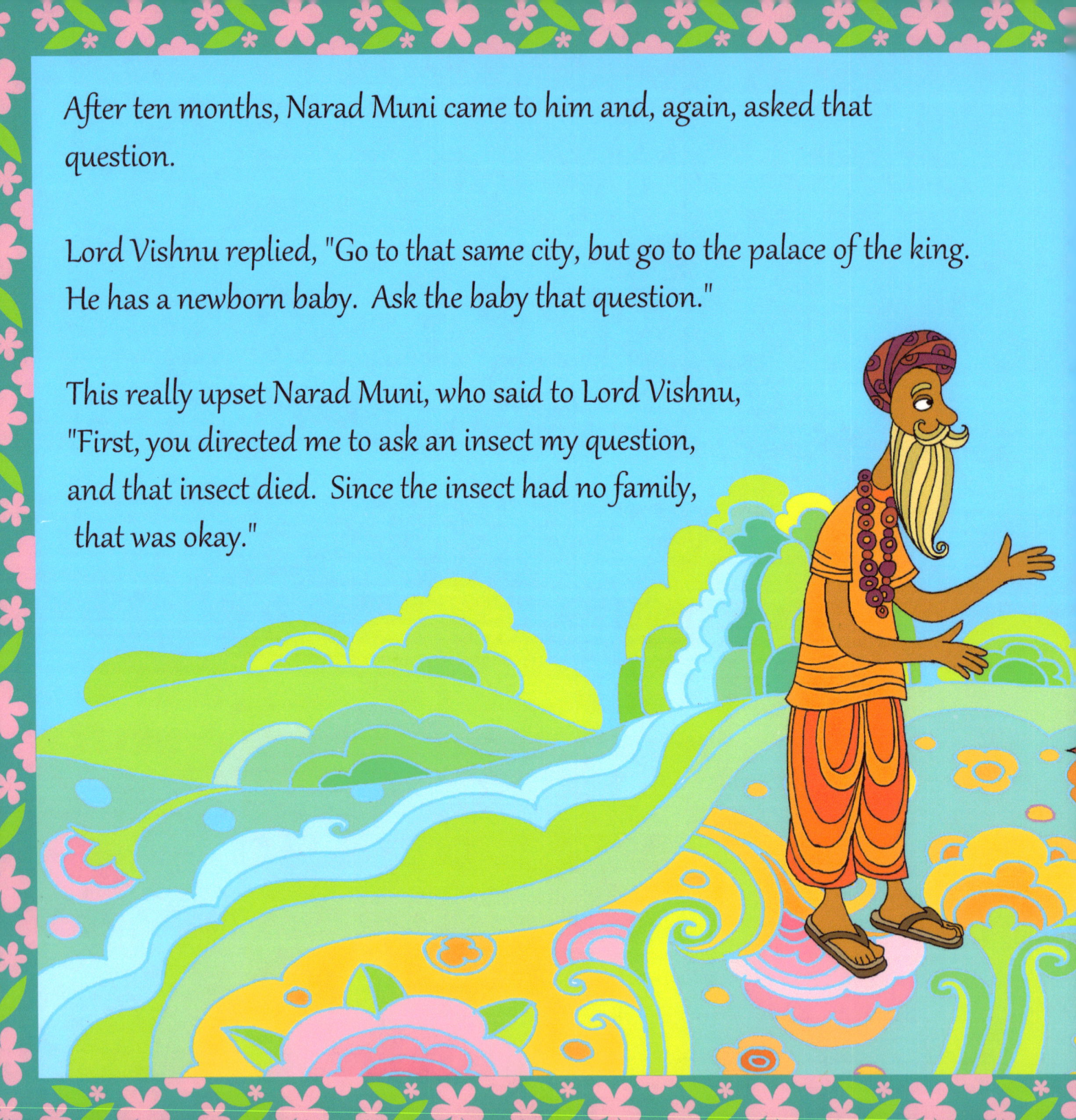

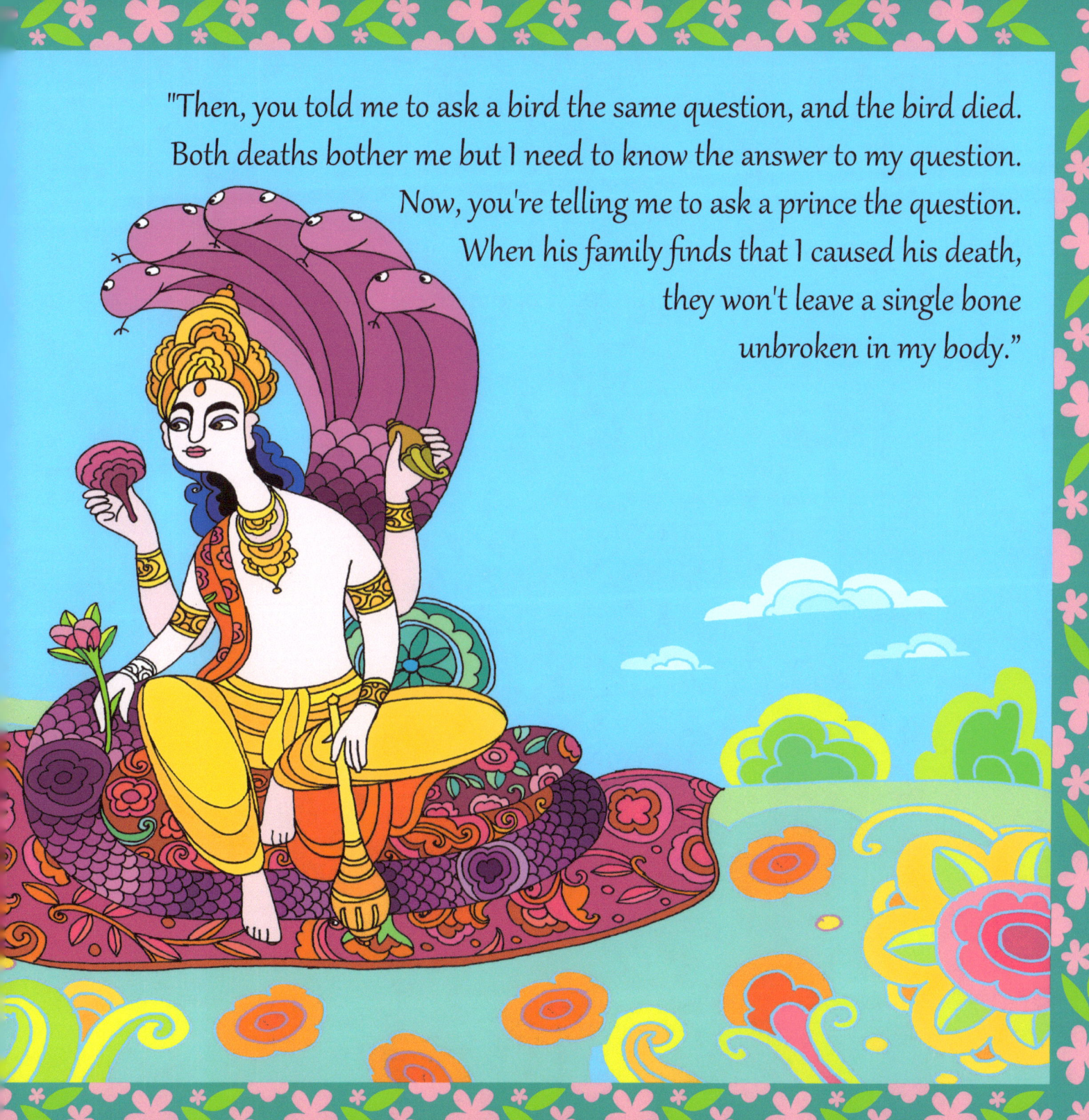

"Then, you told me to ask a bird the same question, and the bird died. Both deaths bother me but I need to know the answer to my question. Now, you're telling me to ask a prince the question. When his family finds that I caused his death, they won't leave a single bone unbroken in my body."

But Lord Vishnu told him, "No, you will get a lot of respect there. Go to the palace and ask your question."

Narad Muni agreed. He travelled to that city, got directions for the palace and then proceeded to the court of the king.

The king was delighted that Narad Muni was visiting his kingdom and asked why he had come. Narad Muni said, "I understand you have a one-month-old baby. I would like to talk to him privately."

The king thought that his baby was very fortunate, because Narad Muni himself had come to meet and talk to him. The king took Narad Muni to the baby's room and left them.

When Narad Muni and the baby were alone, Narad Muni was scared to ask his question. But, nevertheless, he asked him with folded hands, "Oh baby, tell me. What is the benefit of meeting a sadhu?"

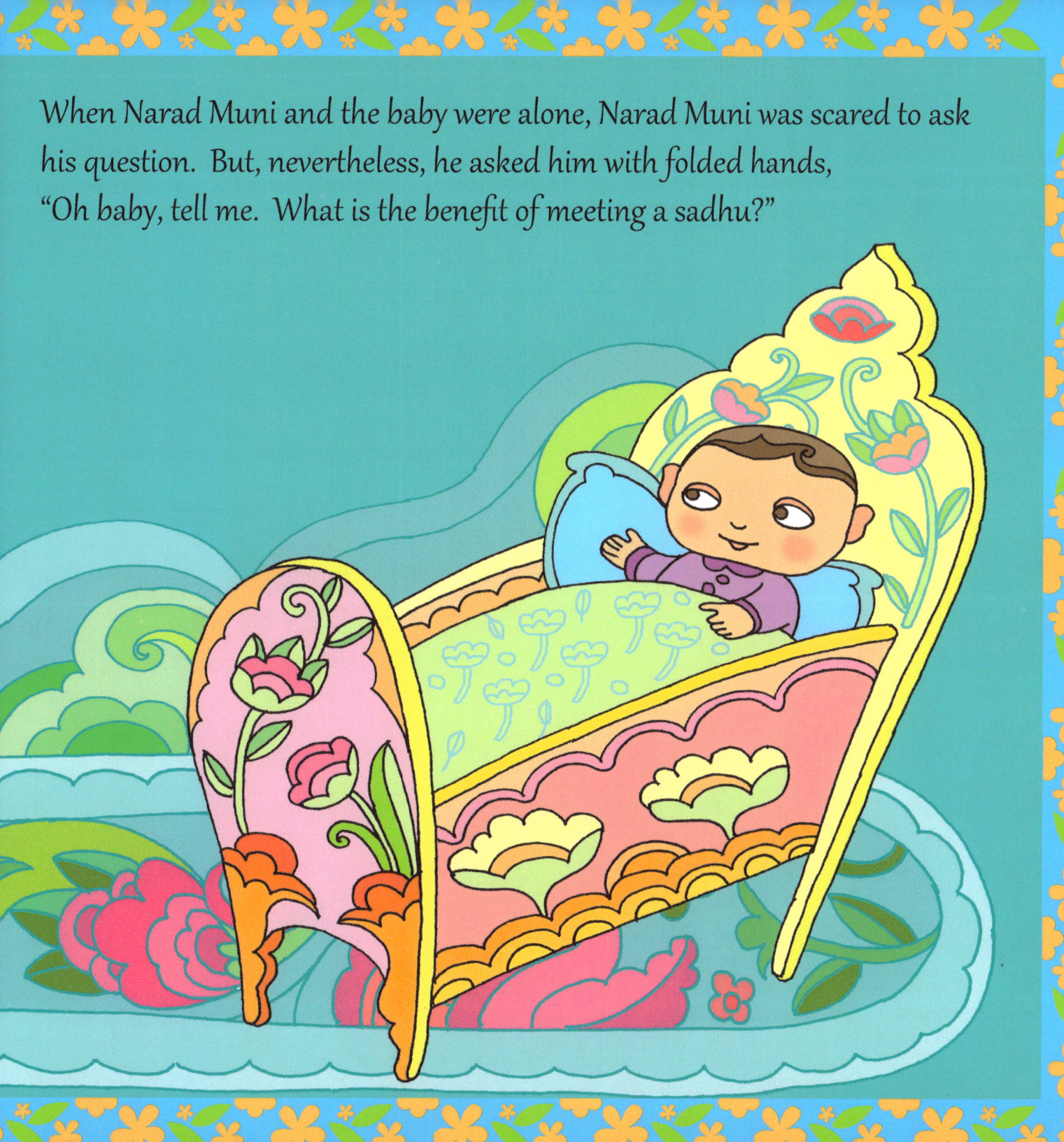

The baby replied, "First, you came when I was that insect. When I saw you and got your darshan, all my karmas of that life were redeemed immediately. That life form ended and I was born with better karmas as a swan."

"Then, you visited me when I was that swan. Again, my karmas for that life were redeemed by your darshan. As a result, with the good deeds and good karmas of having met you, I was reborn as a prince in this kingdom."

"And now, you have come again to visit me and give me your darshan, which redeems all my karmas and my soul can go to heaven or Vaikuntha."

After the prince stated this, he died, and the agents of Vaikuntha arrived to escort his soul back to heaven.

Although Narad Muni was happy for the soul of the baby, he was quite frightened, not knowing how the king would respond to the soul of his son departing the body.

Narad Muni slowly opened the door and approached the king. When he narrated the entire story, the king felt happy, because he knew that someday, he would receive the blessings of Lord Vishnu for having played a part in the salvation of his son's soul.

The king showed even greater respect to Narad Muni after hearing the story and Narad Muni came to know what is the benefit of the company of a sadhu.

Tulsi Sahib says, "If we are able to meet a Master, the karmas of tens of millions of our lives are redeemed, because of the company of the Saints."

Other Books Adapted From Satsangs Given By Sant Ram Singh Ji

www.ingramcontent.com/pod-product-compliance
Lightning Source LLC
Chambersburg PA
CBHW041228040426
42444CB00002B/90